Book A

A Complete Course for Key Stage 3 Religious Studies

CONNECTIONS

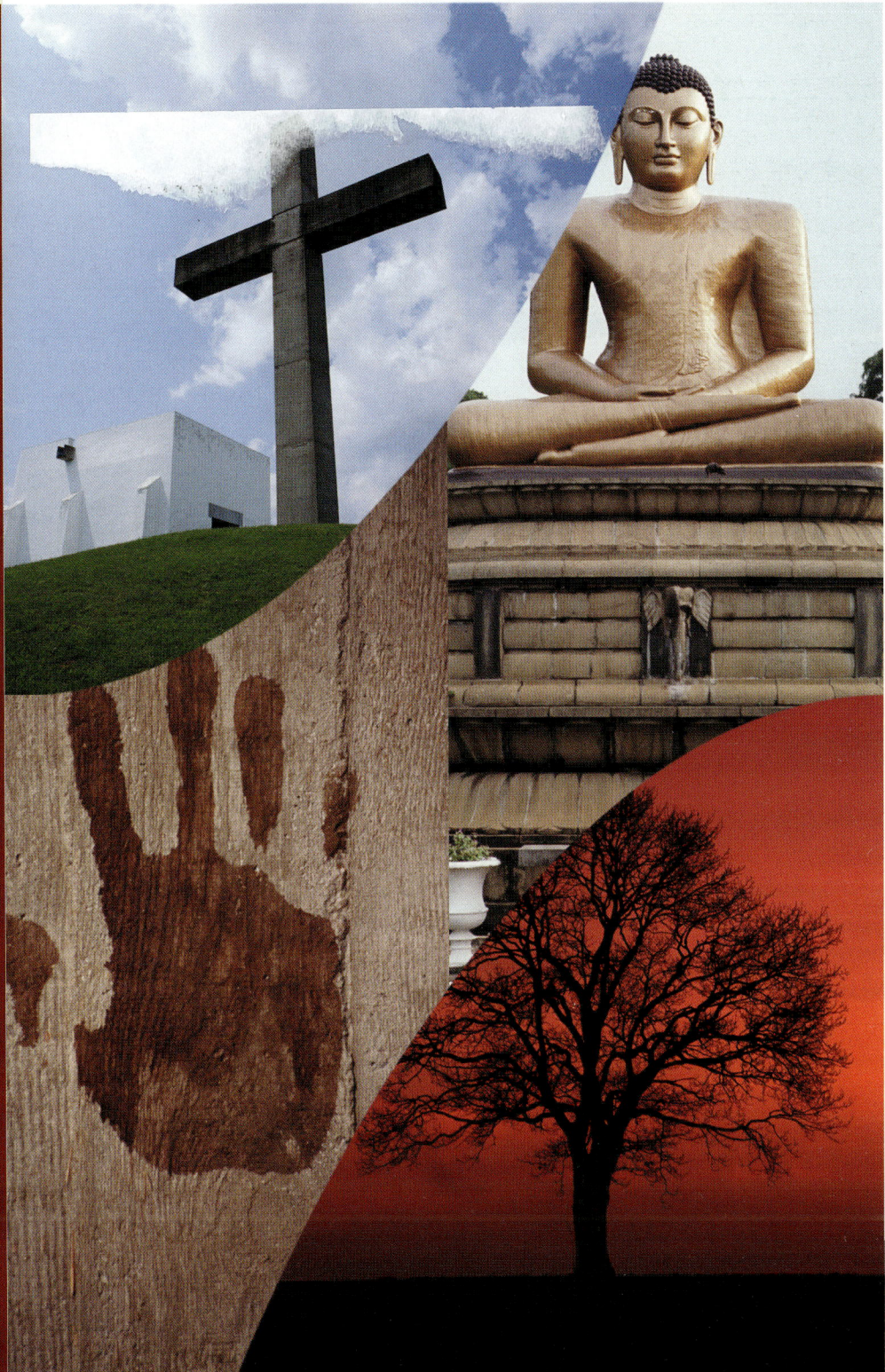

Foundation Edition

Libby Ahluwalia, Ann Lovelace, Jon Mayled, Joe Walker, Joy White

Hodder & Stoughton

A MEMBER OF THE HODDER HEADLINE GROUP

Acknowledgements

The publishers would like to thank the following individuals, institutions and companies for permission to reproduce copyright images in this book:
Cover photos reproduced courtesy of Photodisc.
Associated Press/Dexter Cruez, p55 (top right); Nigel Cattlin/Holt Studios International, p4 (middle, centre row); Bruce Coleman, p4 (right, centre row); Bruce Coleman collection/Marie Read, p4 (left, bottom row); Bruce Coleman/Kim Taylor, p4 (middle, top row); Bruce Coleman/Pacific Stock, 4 (left, centre row); CIRCA Photo Library/John Smith; Corbis, p40; Corbis/Dave Houser, p4 (top right); Corbis/David and Peter Turnley, p20; Corbis/David Samuel Robbins; p54 (top left); Corbis/Gavin Rowell, p54 (bottom right); Corbis/Jack Fields, p55 (left); Corbis/Carmen Redondo, p44; Corbis/Flip Schulke, p23; Corbis/James L Amos, p61 (bottom); Corbis/Jeremy Homes, p42 (bottom left); Corbis/Luca I. Tetton, p42 (top left); Corbis/Michael S Lewis, p29 (bottom left); Corbis/Nik Wheeler, p6; Corbis/Sergio Dorantes, p29 (top left); Corbis/William Dow, p7; Corbis/Wolfgang Kaehler, p29 (top & bottom right), 58; Corbis/Earl & Nazima Kowall, p30; Corbis/Howard Davies, p2 (centre); Corbis/Kevin R Morris, p43 (top right); Corbis/Lindsay Hebberd, p54 (bottom left); Corbis/Philip Gould, p21; Corbis/Tim Page, p55 (bottom right); Life file, p2 (top left, top right, middle, bottom centre & bottom left), 4 (top row left, top right centre row), 42 – 43 (centre), 43 (bottom right), 61 (top); Ruth Nossek, 60; Peter Sanders, p32; Hodder Religious, p22; Photodisc, p9, 60; Popperfoto, p36 © Adrees Latif/Reuters, 53 (top left) © Ian Waldie/Reuters; Science Photo Library, p5; Still Pictures, p14 (top & bottom), 24, 59, 62; Werner Forman, 54 (top right); www.worldreligions.co.uk, 53.

The publishers would also like to thank the following for permission to reproduce material in this book:
Extract from Desmond Tutu *Crying in the Wilderness: The Struggle for Justice in South Africa*, Continuum, published by permission of The Continuum International Publishing Group Ltd; Biblical quotations taken from the *Holy Bible, New International Version*, © 1973, 1978, 1984 by International Bible Society, used by permission of Hodder & Stoughton Ltd, all rights reserved; Extract from Jackie Pullinger *Chasing the Dragon*, Hodder & Stoughton, reproduced by permission of Hodder & Stoughton Limited. Extracts from *The Meaning of the Holy Qur'an* translated by 'Abdullah Yusuf 'Ali, reproduced with permission from Amana Publications, 10710 Tucker Street, Bettsville, Maryland USA.
Every effort has been made to trace and acknowledge ownership of copyright. The publishers will be glad to make suitable arrangements with any copyright holders whom it has not been able to contact.

Orders: please contact Bookpoint Ltd, 130 Milton Park, Abingdon, Oxon OX14 4SB. Telephone: (44) 01235 827720. Fax: (44) 01235 400454. Lines are open from 9.00 - 6.00, Monday to Saturday, with a 24 hour message answering service.

British Library Cataloguing in Publication Data
A catalogue record for this title is available from the British Library

ISBN 0 340 80485 8

First Published 2002
Impression number   10 9 8 7 6 5 4 3 2 1
Year   2007   2006   2005   2004   2003   2002

Printed in Italy for Hodder & Stoughton Educational, a division of Hodder Headline Plc, 338 Euston Road, London NW1 3BH.

CONTENTS

Why do so many people around the world believe in God? They know that God can't be seen. But because they believe in God, this might affect …

…the things they eat

R. B. HALAL FOOD CENTRE
FRESH HALAL MEAT & POULTRY
34   Tel: 0181 – 672 5636   34

…the way they dress

…the careers they choose

…what they do at weekends

…how they spend their money

…the way they bring up their children

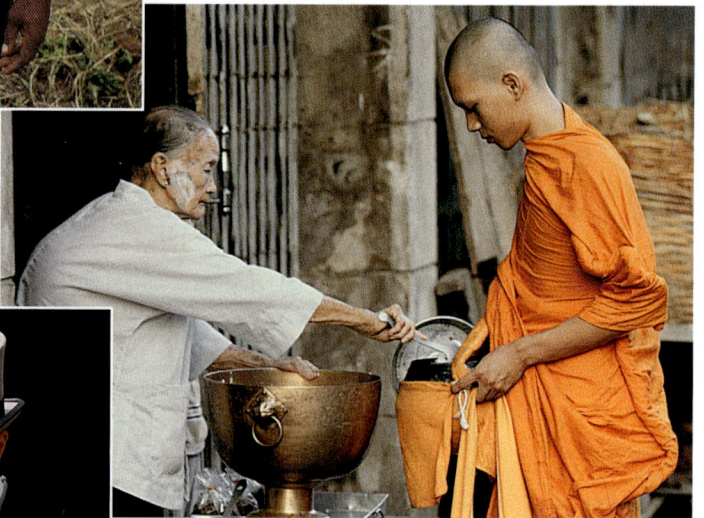

…whom they marry

People who believe in God are called theists. But why do they think they are right, and that there really is a God?

Language for Learning

agnostic – an agnostic is someone who does not know whether there is a God or not.

atheist – an atheist is someone who doesn't believe in God

theist – a theist is someone who believes in one God or many gods

STOP & Think

➤ Make a list of ways in which theists behave and think differently from people who are not religious at all. You might use the pictures to help you think of some ideas.

text message........

We believe things for different reasons.

Sometimes it is because we have worked it out. Sometimes we think we have proof. Some things are just a matter of personal opinion.

People don't agree about where religious belief fits in. Some say we can prove there is a God. Some say we can use our reason to work it out. Some people say that believing in God is a matter of opinion.

action INTO

❶ Look at the following statements. Some are true, and some are false:

a The Eiffel Tower is in Paris.

b Blue is the best colour for a school uniform.

c It is raining today.

d It is wrong to eat meat.

e 2 x 7 = 14

f Skiing holidays are more fun than beach holidays.

g J. K. Rowling is a better writer than Shakespeare.

h Tomorrow will be Wednesday.

Which ones do you think are true, and which ones are false? Compare your answers with the person sitting next to you.

❷ Looking back at your answers to question 1 – *how did you know* whether the statements were true or false? Could anything make you change your mind about these statements?

The Big Picture

Does God exist? Why do people believe there is a God? In this unit, we will be looking at some of the reasons, and seeing why some people are sure there is a God while others are just as sure that there isn't.

Many theists believe that the world shows that God exists. We do not have to guess whether or not God might exist, because there is evidence.

In nature, we can see many examples of beautiful shapes, colours and patterns. These do not look as if they just happen to have fallen into place; they look as though someone deliberately designed them that way, making them beautiful on purpose.

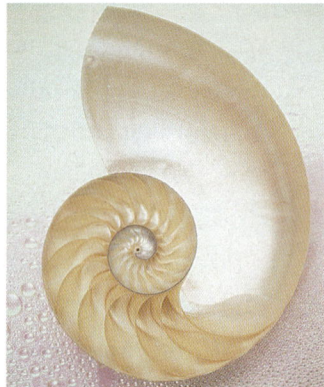

Nature is often beautiful. It can also seem to be very clever. Some parts of nature seem to be just right for the job they do.

A pelican's beak is just right for catching fish...

The cactus and the camel are made so that they can hold water in hot, dry climates...

Polar bears have thick warm white fur to keep out the cold and to hide them in the snow...

Even the planets move around in patterns, as though someone very clever designed their movements.

Theists often argue that this can't have happened just by chance. They say that the world shows that someone designed it, and this is God.

✋ STOP & Think ❓

➤ Can you think of any other examples from nature of plants or animals that seem to be very cleverly designed?

➤ What do you think about the Design Argument? Do you agree with it, or disagree with it?

➤ What are the strong points and the weak points of this argument? Do you agree that nature shows there must be a God who designed it all?

text message.........

Sometimes people use the example of the human eye, to support their view that there must be a God. They talk about how the eye works just like a camera, so that we can see. They say that God must have designed our eyes. They couldn't have just happened by chance.

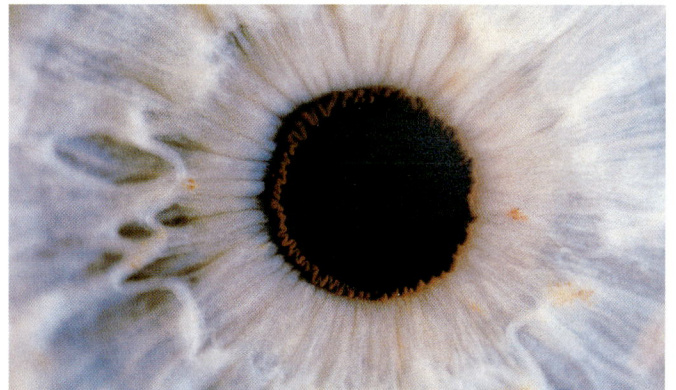

The writers of the Bible sometimes wrote about the beauty and design of the world. For example, in Psalm 19, the writer says that everyone can see the sky and tell from it that God exists. It is as though the sky has a voice and can speak about God for itself:

The heavens declare the glory of God; the skies proclaim the work of his hands.
Day after day they pour forth speech; night after night they display knowledge.

(Psalm 19:1–2)

⏸ PAUSE & RECORD 💿

• Make a collection of pictures from magazines or the Internet which show the beauty of nature, and the ways that animals and plants seem to have been designed. Make them into a collage poster, with the title 'Is there a God who designed all this?'.

When events are called natural disasters, it means that a tragedy has happened because of nature, such as an earthquake, a typhoon, a flood, a drought or a storm. It would not be a natural disaster if people were to blame for it or nobody was hurt.

So a natural disaster is something caused by nature, which produces damage and suffering.

A natural disaster, such as an earthquake, is caused because of the structure of the world. Some people say that if God designed the world, he didn't design it very well.

Some people think that because natural disasters happen, this means that the world is not designed very well after all. Perhaps it means that the God who designed it is not very clever, or not very kind. What sort of a God would make a world where earthquakes and volcanoes kill innocent people? Or perhaps natural disasters mean that there is no God at all.

What about things that are badly designed?

Sometimes, people say that nature can be very cruel. For example, there are many animals which only survive by killing and eating other animals. They look out for the weakest animals to kill, such as the babies. They seem to have been designed to be cruel.

Also, fossils show that some animals died out long ago. Does this mean that God sometimes made designs which were mistakes, and did not work very well?

They also say that some parts of nature are bad, not good, such as old age and disease. Do these really suggest that there is a God who made it all happen? What about people who do really evil things – did God design the world so that some people are good and others are bad?

text message.........

The Design Argument has weaknesses, because not everything in the world is beautiful or good. If we try to look at nature to see if God exists, it can suggest that God does not care whether people or animals suffer. Or it can suggest that God makes mistakes and designs things badly, or that God has no control when things go wrong.

The Cosmological Argument

Sometimes people say that they know God exists, just because the universe exists and everything around us is moving and changing all the time. Theists sometimes say that nothing would exist unless something or somebody had made it. The universe exists; so there must be someone who made it, which must be God. This is known as the **Cosmological Argument** – the cosmos is another name for the universe.

Most of the world's religions say that the universe exists because God made it:

And among his signs is the creation of the heavens and the Earth.

> *(Surah 30:22, from the Qur'an, the holy book of the Muslim religion)*

The earth is the Lord's, and everything in it,
the world, and all who live in it
For he founded it upon the seas
and established it upon the waters.

> *(Psalm 24:1–2, from the Bible, the holy book of Jews and Christians)*

God is the beginning and end of everything. He is the Designer and Creator.

> *(Guru Gobind Singh, a holy teacher from the Sikh religion)*

Most theists believe that there must have been something which started off the whole universe. There must have been a beginning. It had to be made by something with great power. Theists say that God is omnipotent, which means all-powerful – there is nothing that God cannot do.

Language for learning

cosmology – the study of the universe

omnipotent – all-powerful, able to do anything at all

STOP & Think

➤ Imagine a domino standing on its end on a table. The next moment, it is lying down flat. What do you think must have happened to make the domino fall over? Could it have fallen over if nothing had happened at all?

The Cosmological Argument says that things only move when they have been moved by something else. If nothing moves them, then they just stay still and do nothing. The universe is moving. The planets move in their orbits. The universe is getting bigger. What started all this movement? We know that nothing starts moving unless something else is making it move – so, some people say, this shows there must be a God who made it all move.

Does this argument work?

Some people disagree with the Cosmological Argument. They say that perhaps the universe had no beginning. Maybe it has always been here. Perhaps things can just start moving or begin by themselves. Some scientists think that this can happen.

Sometimes atheists say that God is an old-fashioned idea. Atheists say that religious people use the idea of God to explain things that they don't understand, when they should be trying to find out the answers.

But theists argue that when scientists learn about the world, it helps them to learn more about God as well.

Many people say that science can explain how the universe works. But it can't explain why there is a universe at all.

Other people think that there is no reason for our existence. The universe happened by accident. We are only here because of chance. There is no need to look for God to explain anything.

text message.........

Scientists usually believe that the universe was started when there was an explosion - the Big Bang, causing matter to fly out in all directions. As the matter cooled down it formed the stars and the planets, which began to move because of gravity. Some scientists think that this explanation of how the universe began tells us everything. There is no need to bring God into it. Others think that we still need to know what made the Big Bang happen in the first place.

RewindRewindRewind

Look back at the Design Argument. Do you think it is stronger or weaker than the Cosmological Argument? Or do you think they are both strong, or both weak?

Theists say that it is possible to learn about God from looking around us. But they also believe that God makes himself known to some people in a more personal way. Some people say that they know God exists, because they have met him. They have also heard stories of other people who have experienced God. They think that these people can be trusted to be telling the truth.

Some people say that they have seen God in **visions**.

There was a shining light, and I saw a figure stretching her hands towards me and telling me not to be frightened.

Sometimes people say that they have **heard God speaking** to them as a voice.

I didn't know what I should do as a career, but one day I heard a voice telling me that I should become a nurse and go and work in a poor country. So that's what I did.

Some people have had **conversion experiences**, where they have become convinced that God exists, and this has changed their way of life.

I suddenly felt as though a huge weight had been lifted from me, and I felt a great warmth which I knew was the love of God. From then on I became a different person, and now I go to church every Sunday.

Sometimes people believe that through **meditation** they have come to a deeper understanding of God.

After I had been quiet for a long time, I began to realise that all the people, plants and animals are somehow connected together as parts of nature.

Sometimes people feel especially **close to God**, for example when they are in trouble, or when they are in a special holy place, or when they are alone.

Whenever I've got worries about money or about my children, I go to the mosque. I feel that I can talk to Allah when I'm there, and I know Allah listens to me.

Sometimes people believe that they have experienced God through being **healed**, or through receiving **answers to prayer**.

I didn't know what to do when my mother was so ill. I prayed about it every day, asking God to stop her suffering. In the last days of her life she seemed much more peaceful, and even though she died, I knew that God had answered my prayers by taking away her pain.

A lot of these religious experiences are very personal. Only the person who had the experience felt it happen. These experiences are hard to put into words. But people who have these experiences are often sure that God exists.

Language for learning

conversion – when someone completely changes his or her thinking and way of life, often because of a religious experience

Does religious experience prove anything?

If someone has an experience that they think has come from God, it can be very powerful. But other people might be less sure. They might think that it was all a dream. They might think that it is all in the imagination. Religious experiences are too private to prove anything, because no one can test them to see if they really happened, or if they really came from God. But even if they can't prove anything, they can still be useful. If lots of people feel the same way it might suggest that there is more to it than just imagination.

STOP & Think

➤ What would you think if your best friend told you that he or she had experienced God in some way?

11

What do you know?

❶ What do the following words mean: **atheist   theist   agnostic**?

❷ In your own words, explain what the Design Argument says.

❸ Why do some people disagree with the Design Argument?

❹ What reason does the Cosmological Argument give for the existence of God?

❺ Why do some people disagree with the Cosmological Argument?

❻ What do people mean when they say that they have had a religious experience?

❼ How might a religious person's lifestyle be different from the lifestyle of someone who wasn't religious?

❽ Is it possible to prove that there is a God, or to prove that there isn't?

What do you think?

Copy the chart below, filling in the blank boxes below to show whether you agree or disagree with these reasons for belief in God. Try to give a reason for your views.

Reasons people give for belief in God:	My opinion:
Everything in the world seems to be so well suited to its purpose that there must be someone who designed it that way.	
Some people say that they have seen or heard God directly, and they would not say this unless it were true.	
We all have a sense of right and wrong, so there must be a God who tells us what to do.	
There must be a God who rewards us in heaven if we behave well, or punishes us if we behave badly. Otherwise there would be no point in leading a good life.	
The universe exists, so there must be a God who started it off. It could not have just started by itself from nothing.	

action INTO

❶ Make a questionnaire to use with your friends, teachers or family. Ask questions which try to find out whether people believe in God, and their reasons why or why not. Try your questionnaire on four or five different people, and think of a way in which to present your results.

❷ Make a poster to illustrate different views about whether or not there is a God. Divide your page in half – on one side, write 'There must be a God, because...'. and on the other side 'There can't be a God, because...' Use writing and illustrations to show different reasons for or against belief in God.

❸ Design and act out a role play where different people exchange views about whether or not God exists. Think of some interesting characters – an astronomer? Someone who takes emergency aid to the victims of natural disasters? A priest? A scientist?

❹ Find out more about people who claim to have had religious experiences. You might research one of the following:

St Bernadette	**Guru Nanak**
Muhammad ﷺ	**John Wesley**
Julian of Norwich	**Isaiah**

Justice?

Cameron got up for school. He helped his little brothers get ready. He made their breakfast. Mum was still sleeping. Still drunk. Dad was still out. On the way to school one brother said, 'I've forgotten my reading book'. Cameron went back and got it. He made sure the boys weren't late. Dad would thump them if they were. Cameron got to his own school. He was really tired. He went to History. Mr Thomas asked where his pencil was. Cameron had forgotten it. Mr Thomas shouted at him: "Why bother coming to school without a pencil? You stupid boy!" Cameron just kept quiet.

It's not fair!

How many times have you said that? An injustice is when something's not fair. Justice is when you are treated 'right'. It means you get treated fairly.

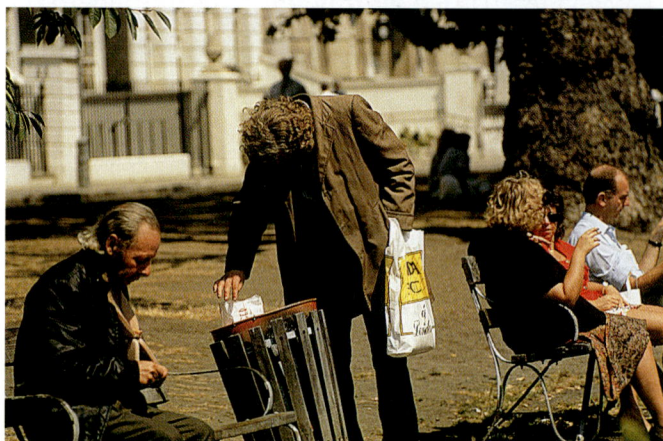

✋ STOP & Think ❓

➤ **Was Mr Thomas being fair?**

⏸ PAUSE & RECORD 💿

• **You are Mr Thomas's Head Teacher. You hear about what he's said. What would you say to him?**

Jesus on justice

Zacchaeus lived in Jesus' time. Zacchaeus was a tax-collector. No one liked him. Jesus came to his town one day. Zacchaeus thought it would be fun to go and see him. There was a big crowd. Zacchaeus couldn't see.

He was very short. He was getting pushed around. What was he thinking?...

They say Jesus is God's son. They say he does amazing things. Yeah, he's a fake. Maybe I can learn a trick or two. Stop pushing me! Stupid people! I work for the Romans. Someone has to. So what if I take some money for myself. Why not? I can't even see Jesus. I'll climb this tree. Now I'm above them all. Just as it should be. Peasants! Here's Jesus. Whoops, he's looking at me. So's everyone else. He's going to moan at me, I know it. But he doesn't. He shouts, 'Come down Zacchaeus!' Who told him my name? 'I shall come to your house for tea tonight.... my friend'. Friend? I feel a bit ashamed. He treats me nicely. Like he cares about me. Yes, he will come to my house. I think I do have something to learn from Jesus.

Jesus went to Zacchaeus' house. He was kind to Zacchaeus. He treated him fairly. Zacchaeus changed completely!

✋ STOP & Think ?

➤ What do you think Zacchaeus' enemies would have thought of all this?
➤ Should Jesus have been kind to Zacchaeus?
➤ Why was Zacchaeus so happy with Jesus?
➤ Make up your own TV news report on the Zacchaeus story.

Dear Paul...

Who was Paul?

Some of the very first Christians had a hard time. They were sometimes killed. Paul didn't like them. But one day Jesus appeared to Paul when he was on the road to a city called Damascus. Then Paul became a Christian himself! He wrote letters to the new Christians. He tried to show them how to be good Christians. These letters are now in the Bible. What would Paul say about justice today?

Dear Paul,

Someone at school is calling me names. Should I get my big brother to hit him?

Ben (12)

Dear Ben,

I was once in prison. But God opened the doors for me. The prison officer was really scared. He nearly killed himself! He'd hit me before he put me in jail. Should I have hit him back? I didn't. We talked. He became a Christian. Talk with the boy at school. Tell him you could have got your big brother to sort it out. But you didn't…

(See Acts 16:16–40.)

Dear Paul,

The boys in my class won't let me play football. It's cos I'm a girl. But I'm just as good as them.

Alice (11)

Dear Alice,

In my time, some men weren't nice to women. I told them to treat women just the same as men. Jesus cares for everyone. The boys should be like Jesus. You're human too!

(See Galatians 3:28.)

Dear Paul,

My friend helps at a charity shop. It's for the homeless. He wants me to help. I'm a Christian, but I don't want to help. I think the homeless are just lazy. I should love them, but I can't.

Gavin (13)

Dear Gavin,

You've got a problem! Christians should love everyone. Love is patient and kind. It doesn't judge people. It does good. Show your Christian love. See what happens.

(See 1 Corinthians 13.)

Dear Paul,

There's a boy in my class. He hates me. He makes fun of me. I'm better at sport than him. I'm going to race him. I'll show him! Is that OK?

Gerry (12)

Dear Gerry,

No, it's not OK. You shouldn't try to get back at him. Try treating him kindly. If you make fun of him, people might not like you! Maybe if you're nice he'll feel bad about being horrible to you.

(See Romans 12:17–21.)

Paul on Justice

- Forgive people
- Don't try to 'get them back'
- Treat everyone the same
- Be fair
- Don't judge
- Be kind and loving

How can we tell?

Jesus taught about justice. He used **stories** sometimes. Sometimes he just **showed** what was right. Sometimes he just came out straight and **said** what we should do.

Lots of Christians try to work out what Jesus would do today. Try the following.

Choose the right answer **a**–**d** after you've read the Bible story.

1. Someone's picking on you. You get the chance to 'get him back'. Do you...

   a. *get him and enjoy it?*

   b. *don't get him but still hate him anyway?*

   c. *try to get on better with him?*

   d. *something else?*

   See Luke 6:27–35.

2. A soldier finds an enemy nearly dead on the battlefield. Should he...

   a. *take him to the hospital?*

   b. *ignore him and let him die?*

   c. *kill him right away?*

   d. *something else?*

   See Luke 10:25–37.

3. A man's teenage son gets into trouble with the police. The boy feels bad about it. What should his dad do?

   a. *give his son another chance*

   b. *let him go to jail*

   c. *throw the boy out of the house*

   d. *something else*

   See Luke 15:11–31.

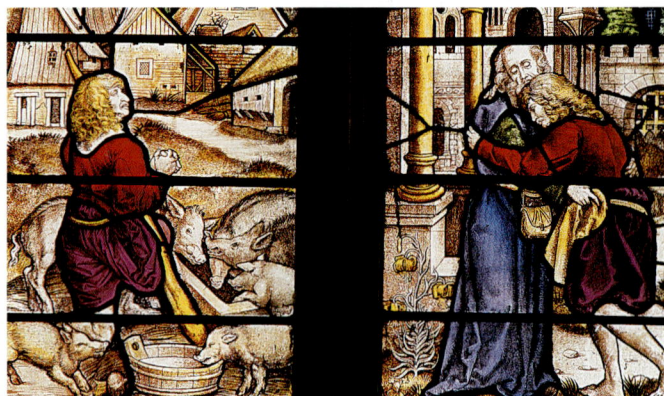

4. A woman wins the lottery. What should she do?

   a. *keep it all*

   b. *give it all away to the poor*

   c. *keep some and give some away*

   d. *something else*

   See Luke 18:18–29.

5. You are a doctor in question 2. You've now got the enemy soldier. What would you do?

   a. *leave him – you've enough to do*

   b. *help him*

   c. *kill him*

   d. *something else*

   See Luke 7:1–10.

Justice for Jesus

Jesus' teaching is hard to follow. This is what Jesus said about justice...

- Don't get your own back on people
- Forgive people
- Use your money to help others
- Treat everyone the same
- Be fair
- Don't judge people
- Be kind and loving

The disciples said:

'When did we ever see you hungry?

When did we not know you?

When did we give you clothes?

When were you sick?

When were you in jail?'

[Jesus said] 'When you did this for anyone, it was like you did it for me.'

Matthew 25:35–46.

RewindRewind**Rewind**

Which two of these points are the same as Paul's on page 17?

You do to me...

Jesus said the following to his disciples. It helps us know what he thought about justice:

[Jesus said to his disciples]

'I was hungry and you fed me. You gave me a drink too.

You didn't know me, but you took me into your home

I had no clothes. You gave me some.

I was sick. You took care of me.

I was in jail. You visited me.'

STOP & Think

➤ **In your own words, what do you think Jesus was saying here?**

19

Desmond Tutu

In South Africa there used to be a thing called apartheid. This meant that black people were treated very unfairly. They couldn't vote. They didn't get paid much. They had to live in poor areas. Desmond thought this was wrong. He became an Anglican Archbishop. This meant he was in charge of many priests. It was a very high position. He fought against apartheid. He thought it was unfair. In 1988 the Government put him in prison.

Eventually apartheid stopped. The new President was Nelson Mandela. He'd been in prison too, but for a very long time. He put Desmond in charge of a committee. This was called the 'Truth and Reconciliation Committee'. It tried to help blacks and whites get on together. During apartheid, lots of bad things had been done. Lots of people wanted revenge. Desmond said this was wrong. People had to forgive. Now Desmond's retired, but he still works hard!

I want a South Africa which is fair. Where everybody has the same chances in life. Where everybody matters.

Desmond Tutu

What does Desmond think about justice?

- God loves everyone just the same
- Everybody should have the same chances in life
- You shouldn't be treated differently just because you're a different colour
- People should care for each other
- The strong should help the weak
- Everyone should have enough money to live a good life
- You should forgive people for what they've done
- You should not get people back for anything bad they've done to you

RewindRewind**Rewind**

Look at Galatians 3:28 (see page 16). Which line might Desmond use to show why he thinks equality is important?

Mother Teresa of Calcutta

Mother Teresa was a nun. She worked in the poor places in Calcutta. She believed everyone matters to God. She treated everyone as if they were Jesus themselves. She started a group of nuns called the Sisters of Charity. They help the sick, the homeless and the dying. Mother Teresa went all over the world to get help for her work. She got money from lots of famous people. But she always went back to Calcutta. She helped the sick and dying herself. She didn't leave it to others. There are Sisters of Charity homes all over the world now. She died in 1996. They might make her a Saint.

When I look after the sick, it's just like I'm looking after Jesus.

Mother Teresa

What did Mother Teresa think about justice?

- Everyone deserves love
- Everyone matters to God
- We should care for everyone
- Nobody is too 'important' to help out
- Everyone deserves the same chances in life
- The strong should help the weak

RewindRewind**Rewind**

Read Matthew 25:35-46 (see page 19) Which line here do you think Mother Teresa might use to say why she helps people?

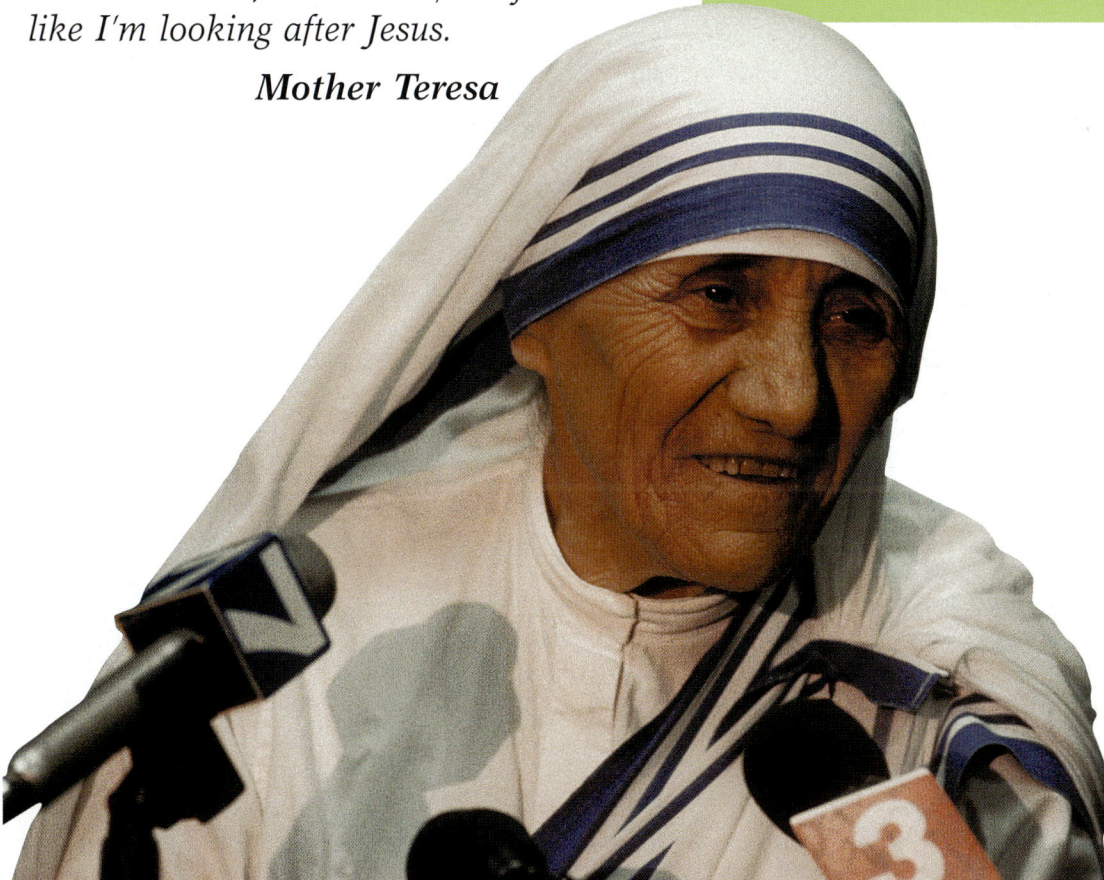

21

Jackie Pullinger

When Jackie was a girl she went to Hong Kong. She lived in a place called the Walled City. This was a very dangerous place. There was lots of fighting. There was lots of crime. It was run by gangs. These were called Triads. In Hong Kong they called the Walled City 'Hak Nam'. This means 'darkness'. Jackie felt really sorry for the people there. She wanted to help them.

She started a little church and a club. Lots of gang members came to the club. They liked Jackie. She cared about them. Lots of them became Christians. They stopped doing bad things. Jackie believes that God loves everyone. If you want to stop doing bad and be good, God will let you. He'll forgive you for the wrong you've done. It doesn't matter how bad you've been.

Jesus loves you. He doesn't love the bad things you've done, but he loves you.

Jackie speaking to one of the gang members

What does Jackie think about justice?

- Everyone should have the same chances in life

- If you agree to change for the better, God will forgive you

- You should show people God's love. It doesn't matter who they are

- You should help the poor to make their lives better.

*Rewind**Rewind***Rewind

Look at the story of Zacchaeus on page 15. Write down one way that Jackie's actions in the Walled City and Jesus' treatment of Zacchaeus are the same.

▐▌ PAUSE & RECORD 💿

- Design a short information leaflet about one of these three Christians. Follow this format:

Side 1

A BIBLE STORY THIS PERSON MIGHT FOLLOW IN HIS/HER WORK	DRAWING OF THE PERSON OR SOMETHING ABOUT THEIR LIFE

Side 2

INFORMATION ABOUT THE PERSON	INFORMATION ABOUT WHAT HE/SHE DOES/DID

Martin Luther King

In the USA in the 1960s, there was a thing called segregation. This was the same as apartheid. Black people weren't allowed in some shops, cafes – even parks. There were signs all over the place – 'Whites only'. Black people even had to give white people their seat on the bus!

Martin thought this was wrong. He helped people protest against it. He was beaten up a lot. He was sent to prison. Some people were killed. Martin said not to fight back. After lots of protest, things changed. Martin's peaceful ways worked. He got justice for the black people.

All through his protests, Martin knew people wanted to kill him. But he wanted justice so he carried on with his work.

On 4 April 1968, someone shot and killed him. But his protests had been very successful.

RewindRewind**Rewind**

Look at Galatians 3:28. Find one line which might explain why Martin did what he did.

What did Martin believe about justice?

- God loves everyone equally
- You should bring justice where there's injustice
- People should get paid fairly
- You should care for everyone
- You should not fight your enemies
- You should show them how to do good
- You should not be treated badly because of the colour of your skin

❚❚ PAUSE **&** RECORD ⊙

- On a display board, split it into four sections. At the top write
'What we think of...'
Then make a section for each of the four people you've looked at in this unit.
Each person in your class should be allowed to write one comment on a piece of card to put on the board.
You don't have to put your name on the cards.

DAILY NEWS

78% OF PEOPLE CAN'T AFFORD TO VISIT A LOCAL GALLERY

THE BIG OPINION
DO YOU GIVE TO THE HOMELESS?

SUNDAY NEWS

RACIST ATTACKS IN SOUTHERN BRITAIN

AVERAGE WAGE STILL HIGHER FOR MALES

Christians think justice is very important. But there's still lots of injustice in the world today. Here are some examples.

Poverty

- 800 million people in the world go to bed hungry every day

- 1.75 billion people in the world don't have safe water to drink

- About 1.3 billion people get paid less than $1 every day

I haven't had a day off for two months. I work from 8am to 10 o'clock at night. Sometimes I work through the night. That's why I get ill.

The bosses cheat us. They say we've only worked about 30 hours a month. It's really 150 hours. But no one writes it down. So the bosses can say what they want.

A Bangladeshi worker

Inequality

- Half the world's population are women. They do 65% of the work. They only get 10% of the wages

- Many black people in the USA say there's still unfair treatment of blacks compared to whites

- Some people think you still get on better in Britain if you're 'posh'

Martin Luther King's dream hasn't come true. There are more black people in prison than white. It's not because we're bad people. If you have a hard life you might turn to crime. Lots of black people have a hard life.

African American

Homelessness

- 100 million people in the world today are homeless

- 40% of Britain's homeless have no place to live because they were thrown out of their house. This was usually by their parents or other relatives

- About 32 million of the world's homeless are children

I was born on the streets. That's where I'll die. I don't care about myself. But I worry about my little brother. He's only 7. He's not my real brother. I just found him on the street. I look after him. I make some money every day. I beg. I steal. At least we eat every day. Lots of street-kids don't.

Maria, Brazilian street-kid, 13 years old

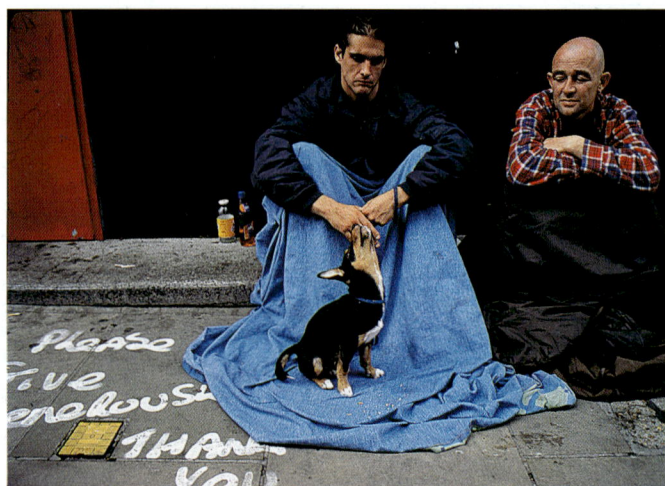

What do Christians do?

Christians work hard to make the world a fair place. They want justice for everyone. They think God wants justice. So they try to make the world the way God wants it to be.

Some Christian organisations work for justice all the time.

Christian Aid – 'We believe in Life before Death'

This organisation started in 1945. It wanted to help people after the war. Now it helps people all over the world. It wants to:

❶ Help people to help themselves.

❷ Challenge the causes of injustice.

❸ Show that everyone can help if they try.

PAUSE & RECORD

- Find out more about Christian Aid. Visit www.christian-aid.org.uk

  Christian Aid
  We believe in life before death

- Find three examples of the work it does and complete the following report.

Country: _____

What's the problem? _____

_____

What is Christian Aid doing to help?

_____

_____

Christian Aid raises money here. It gives it away. It works with partners in poor countries. These people live and work there. They know the best ways to help. In 2000, it raised £57,692,000.

Christian Aid also works to make people think about the poor. This is called campaigning. One campaign was called 'Trade for Life'. This tried to show how buying and selling across the world can harm the poor.

Christian Aid thinks you have to tackle the causes of poverty. Not just the effects. It helps anyone who needs help.

Jo is a Christian Aid volunteer. She says:

I'm a Christian. Jesus always cared for the poor. He told us to love God and our neighbours.

I think 'our neighbours' means people all over the world. That's why I help.

Christian Aid has a statement of Faith. It says:

God puts the poor first. We should love our neighbours. So we should work for justice. We look forward to the time when everyone who works for justice doesn't have to any more.

What do you know?

❶ Complete this sentence. Choose the ending you think is best.

Justice means...

 a. when you get revenge
 b. when you get treated badly
 c. when you get treated fairly
 d. when you go to court

❷ Complete this sentence with your own ending.

Injustice means...

❸ Choose one of the messages below from the Zacchaeus story. Explain, in your own words how the story shows this.

 a. God forgives anyone
 b. Jesus shows we should love everyone
 c. Anyone can change for the better
 d. Everyone matters

❹ Copy and complete:

Paul wrote a letter called _____.
In this he taught about ____. He said that this was _____ and ____. He said it was not _____. Paul said it was the most _____ thing.

[important; kind; patient; Corinthians; selfish; love]

❺ Choose one of the modern Christians you've looked at in this unit. Complete the following:

Name _____

One injustice he/she fought against

was _____

One belief he/she would have about justice is _____

_____

❻ Write one belief about justice which all of the people you've looked at would agree about.

What do you think?

❶ Take some A4 card. Cut it into 24 pieces, each about the size of a credit card.

- On eight of the cards, write one example of a **cause** of injustice in the world today

- On eight of the cards write one example of an **effect** of injustice in the world today

- On eight of the cards write one example of a **response** to injustice in the world today.

Put all the cards together and shuffle them. Pass them to another group to put into the right sections:

cause   effect   response

See which groups can get it right fastest!

❷ Find out more about the people or organisations you've learned about. Using tracing paper, make a 'stained-glass window' poster. This should show the things they do to work for justice.

action INTO

❶ Do a finger puppet show about the Zacchaeus story. At the end, someone should say a few words beginning with: *'The message in this story is...'*

❷ Write a short letter to Christians in your area. This letter should be something like this:

Dear Christians,

We have been thinking about justice in RE time.

We have found that in the world today, there's lots of injustice. Here are some examples _____

_____

_____

We've also found out that Christians are supposed to fight against injustice. This is because _____

_____

We think you should be good Christians and stop injustice. Here are some things we think you should do _____

_____

Yours Sincerely,

Class 7

_____ *School*

❸ Find out how you could help Christian Aid. Maybe you could organise an event at your school.

Final Thoughts

This unit has been about justice. What can you do to make the world a more just place. Copy and complete the following:

To make the world a more just place...

❶ I could . . . .

❷ I could . . . .

❸ I could . . . .

Answer these:

In this unit:

    a. What have you enjoyed best?
    b. What did you not enjoy?
    c. How good was your work?
    d. What would you like to do better?

Now think of three questions about justice that you still have.

Most religions have a founder. A founder is someone who starts something – your school may have a founder. Sometimes people have a special celebration every year called Founder's Day.

In religions, a founder is someone who taught people about the religion right at the beginning and explained to them how God wanted them to live their lives.

You may already know about founders of some other religions. Abraham is sometimes called the founder of Judaism because God chose him and told him that if he obeyed God's teachings he would become the founder of a great nation.

Guru Nanak Dev Ji founded Sikhism. Nanak was very religious and very intelligent. He believed that God wanted everyone to follow the same teachings and taught that there was 'no Hindu and no Muslim' – everyone was equal in front of God. He formed a new religion for his followers which was called Sikhism.

There are other founders such as Jesus and the Buddha. Although Jesus could be called the founder of Christianity, Christians believe that he was the Son of God and came to earth in order to teach people about God. The Buddha, was a very religious man who wanted to find an answer to why people suffered. He's the founder of Buddhism.

In this chapter we are looking at the founder of Islam, the Prophet Muhammad ﷺ. The symbol ﷺ which follows the name of Muhammad ﷺ throughout this chapter is in Arabic, the language of Islam. It stands for the words 'Salla-illahu alaiha wa sallam' – 'peace and blessings of Allah upon him'. Muslims say these words each time they mention the prophet's name as a sign of respect.

The life and teachings of Muhammad ﷺ, are very important to Muslims. By learning about Muhammad ﷺ and his teachings we can also learn more about the religion of Islam.

✋ STOP & Think ❓

➤ What is a founder?

➤ What founders can you think of?

➤ Why do you think it is important to know about the founder of a religion?

➤ Explain why Muslims show respect to Muhammad ﷺ by using this symbol after his name.

The teachings of Muhammad ﷺ are very important to Muslims and are followed by people from all over the world.

RewindRewindRewind

What is the difference between founders such as Muhammad ﷺ and Guru Nanak Dev Ji and others such as Jesus?

29

In Arabic, Muslims call God – Allah.

Muhammad ﷺ was the founder of Islam and the Final Prophet. In their statement of belief Muslims say:

'an la ilaha illal lahu wa anna Muhammadar rasulul lahi'

'there is no god but Allah and Muhammad is the messenger of Allah'

It is very important to remember that Muhammad ﷺ is not believed to be God. He was an ordinary man who was chosen by God to receive his message and to teach it to other people.

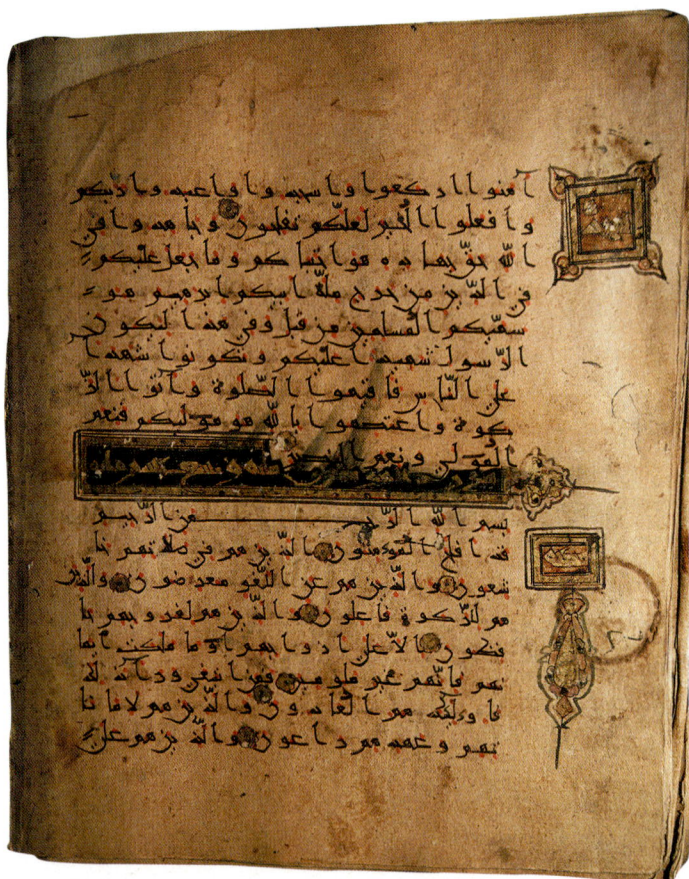

A page from an ancient Qur'an

Muslims never pray to Muhammad ﷺ but they show great respect towards him. The messages which Muhammad ﷺ received are in the Muslim holy book, the Qur'an. Muslims also have the Hadith which has stories about the life of Muhammad ﷺ and his own teachings. When in doubt, Muslims can look at the example of the Prophet and see how he dealt with particular situations.

The birth of Muhammad ﷺ

There are several stories about the birth of Muhammad ﷺ.

Muhammad ﷺ was born in in Makkah which is in Saudi Arabia, in 570 CE. His mother was called Amina and his father, 'Abd Allah. 'Abd Allah died before Muhammad ﷺ was born. On the night that Amina gave birth a large star appeared in the sky. The Prophet's grandfather, 'Abd al-Muttalib spent six days trying to think of a name. On the seventh day he had a dream and was told that the boy should be called Muhammad which means 'The Praised One'. Amina had the same dream.

It was the custom in Makkah to send young children from the city to the oasis at Taif, where there was good food. Women from the desert came into Makkah to collect the young children and to receive money for looking after them.

Because Amina was a widow she did not have enough money to pay for Muhammad ﷺ to go to Taif.

A poor woman called Halima agreed to take the boy. She had a son the same age as Muhammad ﷺ. Halima was very poor and very little would grow on the land on her farm. All she could do was to prayer to Allah for help.

When she reached her farm she found that the fields were full of wheat and the trees were covered in fruit. She had three times as many goats as when she had left and the sheep and camels were producing milk again.

After three years she returned Muhammad ﷺ to Amina.

Three years later Amina died and Muhammad ﷺ had to live with his grandfather 'Abd al-Muttalib.

Two years later, when Muhammad ﷺ was eight, Abd al-Muttalib also died and the boy went to live with Abu Talib, his uncle.

text message.........

Remember: Muslims do not believe that Muhammad ﷺ is God. He was an ordinary man chosen to receive God's message and to teach it to other people. Muslims never pray to Muhammad ﷺ but they show great respect towards him.

STOP & Think

➤ What other birth stories of religious leaders do you know about?

➤ Why do you think these stories are so important to believers?

➤ Why might some people say that Muhammad ﷺ had a very hard life as a child?

Abu Talib was a merchant and took Muhammad ﷺ with him on his journeys. One story tells how they were travelling through Syria, when his uncle met a monk called Bahira.

The monk believed that one day a great prophet would arrive and hoped that he would live to see him.

Bahira had seen the camels approaching and had noticed that a single cloud was travelling with them, just as though it was sheltering someone from the sun.

Bahira invited the merchants to a meal in his cell. Abu Talib said that he had left Muhammad ﷺ to look after the camels. Bahira sent for him and asked him many questions.

He asked Muhammad ﷺ to swear by the gods of Makkah, al-Lat and al-Uzza. Muhammad ﷺ refused. Bahira spoke to Abu Talib and said:

'This child will be a great leader. Take him back to your country and look after him well'.

Muhammad ﷺ worked for his uncle as a camel driver, and was respected by everyone who met him. He was known as al-Amin, the trustworthy one. A wealthy widow, Khadijah heard about his honesty, and employed Muhammad ﷺ to look after her businesses. She asked him to marry her although she was much older than him. Muhammad ﷺ and Khadijah were very happily married. Together they had six children:

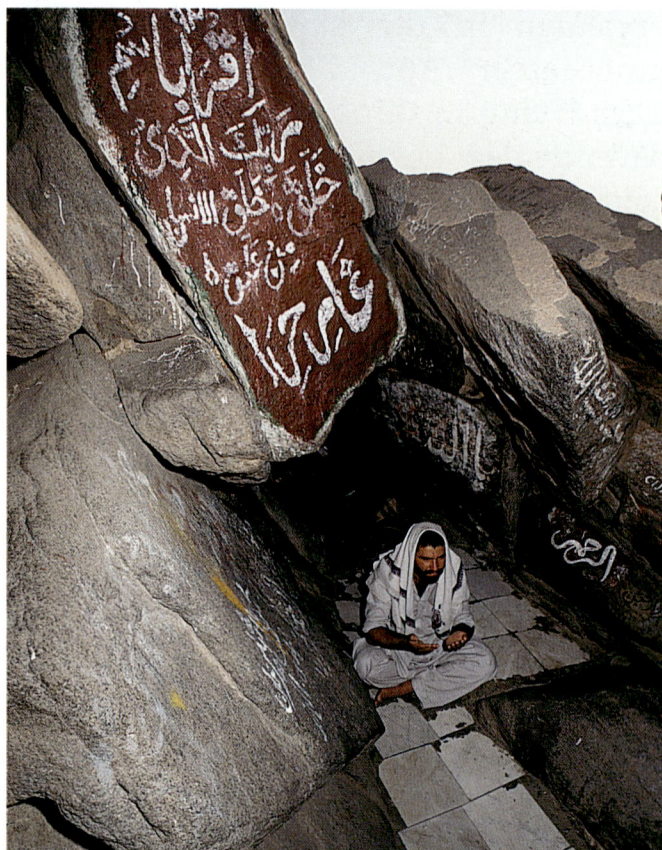

The cave on Mount Nur where Jibril spoke to Muhammad ﷺ.

two sons and four daughters. The two sons both died in childhood, but the daughters survived and themselves were happily married.

Jibril apears to Muhammad ﷺ

Makkah was a busy trading centre. Muhammad ﷺ felt that the people were not living their lives as God would have wanted. He often went into the hills or the desert to sit and pray. One night, in 611 CE, he was sitting in a cave on Mount Nur. He looked up and saw the Angel Jibril (Gabriel). The figure commanded him:

'Proclaim (or Read!)
In the name
Of thy Lord and Cherisher,
Who created —

Created man, out of
A (mere) clot
Of congealed blood:

Proclaim!
And thy Lord
Is Most Bountiful —

He Who taught
(The use of) the Pen —
Taught man that
Which he knew not.'
(Surah 96 Al 'Alaq (The Clinging Clot) or Iqra' (Read!) 2-5

Then the angel said, 'O Muhammad ﷺ you are the messenger of Allah and I am Jibril'.

Muhammad ﷺ could not read or write, so he had to repeat the words spoken to him until he could remember them.

This first night when Muhammad ﷺ began to receive messages from Jibril is called Laylat-ul Qard – the Night of Power.

The next revelation came to Muhammad ﷺ while he was resting at home one night. In this message he was ordered to tell the people of Makkah what he had learnt. Muhammad ﷺ spoke to his cousin 'Ali, his friends Abu Bakr and Uthman and a slave called Bilal (Zayd Bin Haritha) who had been given his freedom by Abu Bakr.

These five were the first Muslims and this small group met together to pray to Allah.

action INTO

❶ Make a chart with two columns.
  • In the first column write down the important events in Muhammd's ﷺ life
  • In the second column write down what you feel have been important events in your life
  • Add further events to the chart as you learn more about Muhammad ﷺ.

text message.........

Bilal was the son of a Christian princess from Yemen who fell in love with an African slave called. Riah. Bilal was their only child.

Bilal wanted to follow the teachings of Muhammad ﷺ but his owner, Umaya would not allow this.

Every day Bilal was taken out of Makkah at noon and made to lie on the sand under the burning sun with a stone on his chest. Bilal refused to give up his faith and eventually he was bought from Umaya by Abu Bakr.

Muhammad ﷺ continued to receive messages from Allah through Jibril for several years.

At first, there were very few people who would listen to his messages. People in Makkah made fun of Muhammad ﷺ and complained about his preaching. They did not want to change their way of worship and were afraid that they would lose money if people did not come to worship the idols in the Ka'bah.

In 622 CE Khadijah died and so did Muhammad's ﷺ uncle Abu Talib.

Muhammad ﷺ leaves Makkah

The people of the city of Yathrib, 480km north east of Makkah, asked Muhammad ﷺ to go there as their governor. There were many Muslims living in Yathrib.

Muhammad ﷺ could not leave Makkah in case he was seen by his enemies. The leaders of an important tribe, the Quraysh, were trying to find a way to kill Muhammad ﷺ. They decided that one man from every group or tribe would wait outside Muhammad's ﷺ house all night and they would all kill him together when he came out in the morning.

That night Jibril appeared to Muhammad ﷺ and warned him not to sleep at home. The prophet asked 'Ali to sleep in his house instead and promised that no harm would come to him.

Next morning, the murderers were shocked when 'Ali opened the door and they realised they had been tricked.

Muhammad ﷺ and Abu Bakr set off on two fast camels. They went south, in order to trick the people looking for them. Later they turned north towards Yathrib.

When they reached a mountain called Thawr, they stopped and hid in a cave. Soon they could hear the men outside. One of them said, 'No-one's been in this cave for a long time because there is a spider's web across the entrance and a dove nesting on the ledge.' Soon the men moved on and left the cave.

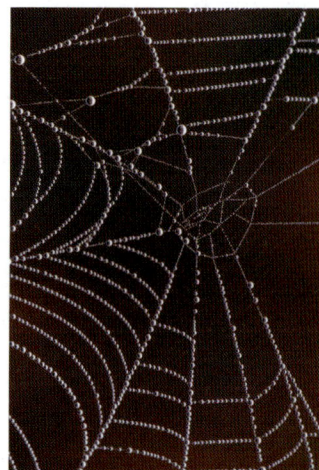

Abu Bakr could not understand, he had not seen the spider or the dove but Muhammad ﷺ knew it was God's work.

After a few days, they continued on their journey to Yathrib and Muhammad ﷺ was welcomed by the Muslims there.

The city was renamed Madinah al-Nabi – City of the Prophet. Today it is known as al-Madinah.

The Hijrah

The Hijrah, or emigration, to Madinah is a very important event for Muslims and is placed at the beginning of the calendar as the first day of the first year of Islam. So the Muslim years are numbered 1 AH, 2 AH (after Hijrah) etc. The Hijrah is known as the birth of the Islamic community.

After Muhammad's ﷺ arrival, the very first mosque was built in al-Madinah. They had to decide how they were going to call people to prayer. One of Muhammad's ﷺ followers, Abdullah bin Zaid, said that he had had a dream in which he heard a human voice calling people to pray.

Muhammad ﷺ decided that this must be God's will and chose Bilal, saying that he had the best voice. Bilal then climbed on to the highest roof and gave the first call to prayer:

Allahu akbar

Allah is the Greatest

I bear witness that there is no god but Allah

I bear witness that Muhammad ﷺ is Allah's messenger

Rush to prayer

Rush to success

Allah is the greatest

There is no god but Allah

action INTO

❶ Try to find out as much as you can about Muhammad's ﷺ life. Use this book and any other information you can find.

❷ Prepare a list of questions which you could use to find out from a Muslim why Muhammad ﷺ was important.
Use the answers from these questions to produce a table.

✋ STOP & Think ❓

➤ Why did Muhammad ﷺ have to leave Makkah?
➤ How did God protect him during his journey?
➤ Why was Bilal chosen to give the Call to prayer?

Living at al-Madinah was not easy. There were many clans amongst the tribes and many battles.

During this time Muhammad ﷺ received more messages from Jibril and in one of these he learnt that Muslims should now pray facing the Ka'bah in Makkah.

In 624 CE Muhammad ﷺ led his followers into a successful battle against soldiers from Makkah. All the Arabs became Muslims whilst the Jews in the area were allowed to continue in their own faith. They fought again in 627 at the battle of al-Khandaq – the trench. This ended with a treaty in 628 and Muslims were free to travel to the Ka'bah in Makkah.

The first Hajj

Muhammad ﷺ led the first pilgrimage to Makkah in 630. As soon as they had entered Makkah, Muhammad ﷺ went straight to the Ka'bah. He rode around it seven times and then destroyed all the idols which were inside and cleaned it.

This event was the first Hajj. The annual pilgrimage to Makkah which is one of the Five Pillars of Islam which all Muslims try to obey. At the end of this first Hajj, Muhammad ﷺ preached a sermon on Mount Arafat.

In this sermon he told the Muslims how they should behave:

Muslim pilgrims pray towards the Ka'bah (the black structure) in the centre of the Gand Mosque in Makkah.

- He said that everyone's property was their own and stealing was always wrong.

- No one was allowed to charge interest if they lent money.

- Husbands and wives must treat each other with respect.

- No Muslim is better than any other Muslim.

- Muslims should follow the teachings of the Qur'an and the example of Muhammad ﷺ.

- People would be judged by Allah to see how well they lived.

- They should worship Allah, pray, fast during the month of Ramadan and pay Zakah (an annual payment to the community).

- People should look after their servants and feed and clothe them well.

- There would be no more prophets after Muhammad ﷺ.

On the same day, Muhammad ﷺ received his last revelation from Jibril:

'This day have I
Perfected your religion
For you, completed
My favour upon you,
And have chosen for you
Islam as your religion.'
Surah 5 Al Ma'idah (The Repast) 3

Muhammad ﷺ died in al-Madinah on 12th Rabi' ul-Awwal (8 June) in 632. When he died, Bilal was so upset that he could not stand and so, for the first time, could not give the call to prayer.

Abu Bakr came out to speak to the crowd:

'People who worshipped Muhammad ﷺ should know that Muhammad ﷺ is dead, but people who worshipped Allah should know that Allah is alive and never dies.'

text message.........

Remember: Muslims believe that Muhammad ﷺ was a prophet, a messenger from Allah. This is different from Christians who believe that Jesus was actually God.

RewindRewind**Rewind**

- What examples did Muhammad ﷺ say that Muslims should follow?

- What did Muhammad ﷺ say about borrowing money?

- What did Muhammad ﷺ say about how Muslims should treat other people?

Islam is the second largest of the world religions and the fastest growing. There are more than eight hundred million Muslims in the world today and they live in every country.

The word 'Islam' means 'submission'. Muslims are people who submit themselves, or follow the will of Allah.

The founder of Islam

Muhammad ﷺ was the founder of Islam, a new religion. Muslims see him as the last in a line of prophets which begins with Adam. Most of the prophets of Islam are found in the Torah – the Jewish Scriptures (and the Old Testament of the Christian Bible) as well as in the Qur'an.

Islam teaches that God tried three times to teach people how they should behave and live a religious life. The first time was to the Jews and then, later, he sent Jesus. However, each time, people changed the message that they had received from God. Muhammad ﷺ was the last of the prophets and there would be no more.

The Qur'an

Muslims believe that the Qur'an is the direct word of Allah given to Muhammad ﷺ by Jibril. No word of the Qur'an has been changed. The Qur'an on earth is just a copy of the real Qur'an which is in heaven.

Muslims follow the teachings of God in the Qur'an and learn from the teachings and life of Muhammad ﷺ which are found in the Hadith.

As well as receiving the Qur'an, Muhammad ﷺ brought peace to the tribes of Arabia. He cleaned the Ka'bah and removed the idols in it and established Makkah as a holy city for all Muslims.

Jerusalem is also a holy city for Muslims. One night, just before Muhammad ﷺ left Makkah for al-Madinah, he travelled with Jibril, on a winged animal called Buraq, from Makkah to Jerusalem and then on through the seven heavens. This is remembered by Muslims as Laylat ul Isra wal Mi'raj.

The Five Pillars of Islam

The way of life which Muhammad ﷺ gave to his followers can be found in the Five Pillars of Islam.

The Five Pillars are visible signs of a Muslim's way of life and the unity of the ummah, the worldwide Muslim community:

- **Shahadah** – the declaration of faith – 'There is no god but Allah; Muhammad ﷺ is the messenger of Allah'.

- **Salah** – prayers five times a day.

- **Zakah** –muslims give 2.5% of their surplus income every year. It helps the ummah (community of Muslims) and is shared for the benefit of everyone. It helps the people who give because they know that they are not being greedy or selfish with their money.

- **Hajj** – the Pilgrimage to Makkah made during the Muslim month of Dhul-Hijjah. This is a duty which every Muslim tries to carry out once in their lifetime.

- **Sawm** – going without food during the hours of daylight for the whole of the month of Ramadan. This helps Muslims to focus on prayer and the Qur'an, to know that they are obeying God and to share this with the rest of the worldwide community of Muslims.

THE FIVE PILLARS

SHAHADAH SALAH ZAKAH SAWM HAJJ

The Five Pillars of Islam

text message.........

All Muslims should live their lives in submission to the will of Allah.

All Muslims should follow the Five Pillars: Shahadah, Salah, Zakah, Hajj, Sawm

RewindRewind**Rewind**

- Where do Muslims say the real Qur'an is?
- What is Sawm?

What do you know?

❶ Where was Muhammad ﷺ born?

❷ What does this symbol mean – ﷺ?

❸ Who was Muhammad's ﷺ first wife?

❹ Who gave the first part of the Qur'an to Muhammad ﷺ?

❺ Who was Bahira?

❻ Write a paragraph about Bilal.

❼ Why did Muhammad ﷺ go to Yathrib – al-Madinah?

❽ What did Muhammad ﷺ do at the Ka'bah in 630?

❾ Where did Muhammad ﷺ give his last sermon?

❿ What are the Five Pillars?

What do you think?

❶ Muslims do not allow pictures of people or animals. They say that pictures like this would be insulting to Allah. Why do you think they believe this?

❷ From what you have read, what sort of person do you think Muhammad ﷺ was?

❸ Think about the rules which Muhammad ﷺ gave his followers in his last sermon. Explain why these are important for Muslims.

❹ Why do you think Allah chose Muhammad ﷺ to be his messenger?

In the mosques decorative geometric patterns are used rather than statues or pictures.

action INTO

❶ Make a chart about founders. You can choose founders of different religions or those of charities, schools or other organisations. For each one, except Muhammad ﷺ, try to find a picture of the founder.

❷ Write a short prayer which thanks God for life and creation and asks God to look after people who are suffering.

❸ Islamic patterns like the one on page 40 are made up from many different geometric shapes like triangles, squares and kites. Using squared paper, design your own pattern and remember not to draw animals or people.

Final Thoughts

In this unit you have learnt about Muhammad ﷺ the founder of one of the world's religions.

What have you learnt about Muhammad's ﷺ life and how he came to be the Prophet of Islam?

Explain how Muhammad's ﷺ life might be a good example for all people today.

Each year millions of people visit the places you see in the pictures. All these places are connected with a special man. He lived over two and half thousand years ago.

Why was he important?

Why do so many people believe he gave a message for all time?

The Temple of the Reclining Buddha – Bangkok, Thailand

Dambulla Rock cave – Sri Lanka

The Temple of the Emerald Buddha – Bangkok, Thailand

Tooth Relic Temple – Kandy, Sri Lanka

Angkor Wat – Cambodia

43

Where and when was Gotama Buddha born?

Just across the border of India is the country of Nepal. It was here, in a village called Lumbrini that Gotama was born. He was given the name Siddattha. His father was a rich king. He asked a wise priest to look into Siddattha's future. The priest said that he would either become a great ruler or a poor holy man. The king wanted his son to be a great ruler like himself.

STOP & Think

➤ How can you tell the person in the picture is special?

➤ What sort of mood do you think he is showing?

➤ What evidence do you have?

The Big Picture

In this unit you will learn:

- Where and when Gotama Buddha was born
- Why he decided to leave home
- How his life changed
- What he taught
- What is important about his teachings for people today.

A life of luxury

The king loved his son. He wanted to protect him and keep him happy. So he made sure that Siddattha had everything he wanted. He lived in a beautiful palace with only beautiful people around him. He never went outside the palace grounds, so he did not know about the world outside. He did not know that there were poor people. Anyone who became ill or old was not allowed to stay in the palace. So Siddattha did not even know that people could get sick or die.

Learning to be a ruler

Siddattha grew up, following in his father's footsteps. He became good at sport and art. A beautiful princess was chosen for him to marry. Soon they had a baby son. And all this time the king made sure that Siddattha had all he wanted. Even though he was now grown up he still did not know what went on in the world outside.

✋ STOP & Think ?

➤ Why did Siddattha's father try and keep him from the outside world?

➤ Do you think having lots of money and luxuries makes people happy?

➤ What else might be needed?

❚❚ PAUSE & RECORD 💿

- Write a list of things Siddattha would not have known about by not going outside the palace.

- Do you think the king was being kind or being cruel by keeping him in? Give a reason for your answer.

In spite of all that was done to make him happy, Siddattha became restless. He wanted to find out about the world outside. So one day he asked his father to let him go out. For the very first time he was going to be taken by chariot into the city.

Imagine how excited he was! He just couldn't believe his eyes at all the things he saw. Everything was so different. His charioteer was called Chanda. Sidattha asked him many questions. Out of all the sights he saw, there were four things that puzzled him most.

A very old and frail person

A person suffering in pain through illness

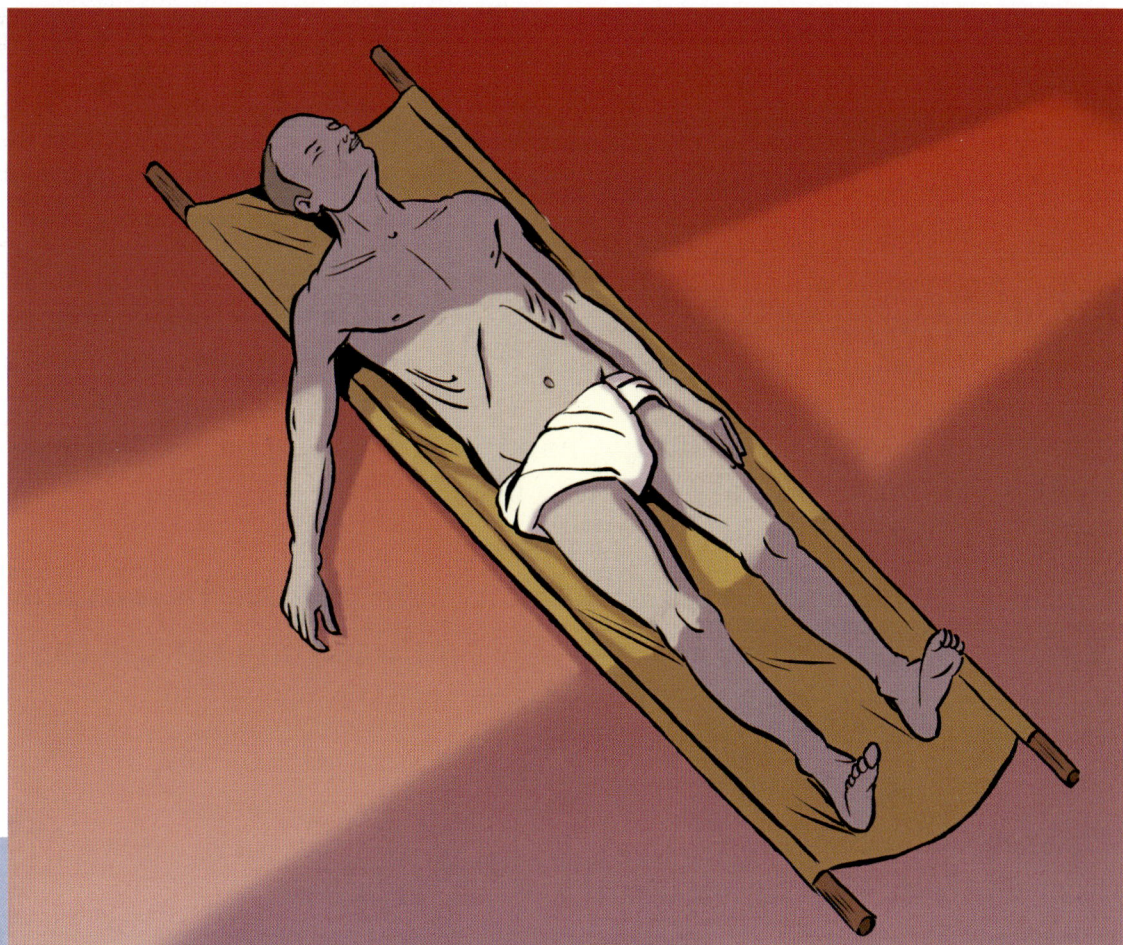

A dead body

A holy man

The journey that changed everything

SIDDATTHA: Don't go so fast, Chanda. There's so much to take in. It's like being in a foreign country.

CHANDA: Your father doesn't want you to be out for too long.

SIDDATTHA: But there's so much to see. I'm going to be king one day. I need to see my people.

CHANDA: But you don't need to see them up close. Your father doesn't want you getting upset.

SIDDATTHA: Stop Chanda! There's someone lying down over there. He's holding his stomach and crying out. What's the matter with him?

CHANDA: He is ill. Everyone can become ill at some time.

SIDDATTHA: But why? What does it mean?

CHANDA: The body can become injured or get a disease. This causes pain.

SIDDATTHA: Why was I never told this? I should have been told.

STOP & Think

➤ Have you ever had to explain something difficult to someone?

➤ Make up a conversation Siddattha might have had with Chanda about one of the other three sights that puzzled him. Try and write what questions he would have asked and how you think Chanda would have answered.

We all have times when we realise something for the first time

Innocent people suffer.

So there's no Father Christmas.

Some people don't have beds.

Life could never be the same again

Siddattha just couldn't forget what he had seen. He was still puzzled. What was the truth about life? Why do people suffer? He just had to find the answers. To do this he would have to leave home. So, leaving behind his riches, he said goodbye to his family and set off.

He travelled to many places. He talked to wise and holy people. He tried living in different ways. He even tried going without food for a long time. Years went by. At last, feeling tired from his travels, he stopped to rest. He sat under a tree to meditate.

The kind of tree that Siddattha sat under is now known as the Bodhi Tree because 'bodhi' means enlightenment.

text message.........

Meditation means thinking very deeply and carefully. It means shutting out all other thoughts and concentrating hard. Many people use meditation to get things clear in their minds.

STOP & Think

➤ Where do you like to sit and think about important things?
➤ Can you think of a question we might never know the answer to?

PAUSE & RECORD

• Think of five examples of people who are given a new name or title after doing something important, e.g. Prime Minister, Hajji.

Siddattha 'sees the light'

After his meditation everything became clear to Siddattha. He understood the truth about life. He knew why there was suffering. This new understanding is called the **enlightenment**. From that time, he was called the Buddha, which means 'The Enlightened One'. After this he would teach others what he had discovered. People still follow these teachings today. They are called Buddhists.

text message.........

Enlightenment is a hard word to explain. We sometimes use it in our everyday lives. It is when we understand something in a different way for the first time. We might then say 'the penny dropped'. The Buddha's enlightenment was about the meaning of life itself.

⏸ PAUSE & RECORD 💿

- Is there something important about life that you believe to be true?

Are you telling me the truth?

Is it true the tooth fairy will come?

I will always be true to you.

These are the truths the Buddha taught us.

Nothing stays the same

We have learned that the Buddha understood the truth (what is true) about life. We can use the word **truth** in different ways.

The kinds of truth which the Buddha taught are important truths about life. They help people see how they can live better lives.

One important truth that came to the Buddha was about **change**. He realised that everything in the world is always changing. Nothing lasts forever. Until people can accept this, they will always suffer.

PAUSE & RECORD

- What things do you know about which change?
- Which ones make you feel sad? Which ones make you feel happy?
- Which changes in your life are you looking forward to?
- Which changes are you not looking forward to?

51

After his meditation, the Buddha started to teach people what he had learned. His first teaching was called **The Four Noble Truths**.

The Four Noble Truths

1. All life has suffering

The Buddhist word for suffering is **dukkha**. It means everything from a small headache to deep sadness. The Buddha said that even happy times can be sad as we know they can't last.

I'm so sad we're going home tomorrow.

2. Suffering comes from wanting

We often suffer because we want what we haven't got. This means we're unhappy because we're never satisfied.

If only I could afford those clothes!

3. When we stop wanting we will stop suffering

We will be happy if we do not envy but are content with what we have. Greed and envy can make other people suffer too.

I don't care about the woman I just want the money.

4. Happiness comes by following the Middle way

The Buddha believed people should not be too rich or too poor. To find a balance between the two, they must take special steps. These steps are called 'The Eight-Fold Path'.

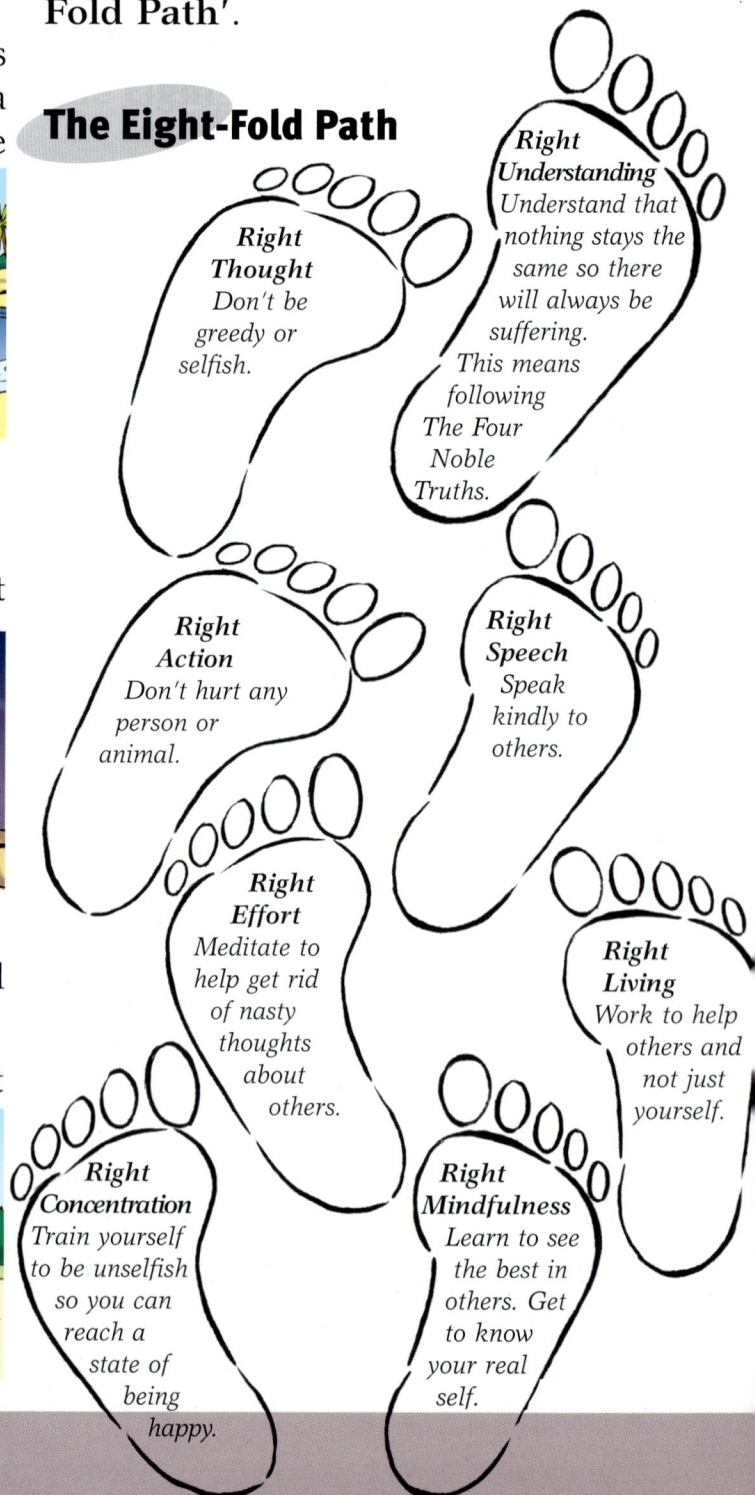

The Eight-Fold Path

Right Understanding
Understand that nothing stays the same so there will always be suffering. This means following The Four Noble Truths.

Right Thought
Don't be greedy or selfish.

Right Speech
Speak kindly to others.

Right Action
Don't hurt any person or animal.

Right Effort
Meditate to help get rid of nasty thoughts about others.

Right Living
Work to help others and not just yourself.

Right Concentration
Train yourself to be unselfish so you can reach a state of being happy.

Right Mindfulness
Learn to see the best in others. Get to know your real self.

Buddhists do not think of the Buddha as a God. They see him as a great teacher and guide. He is a role model for how to live their lives. Many of us have people we look up to. We may try to copy their example. Sometimes they are people from the past we have read or learned about. Or they may be people we know who are living today.

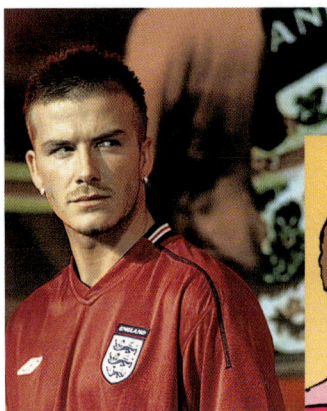

PAUSE & RECORD

- Have you ever felt envy?
- How has it made you feel?
- How have you dealt with it?

Text Message.........

Buddhists believe that if they follow The Eight-Fold Path they will become enlightened. They will have 'blown out' all their feelings of envy and hate. They will see the world in a different way. They will be able to say they have reached a state of peace. The word for this is Nirvana.

STOP & Think

➤ Who are the people who teach and guide you?
➤ Do you have any people you would call role models?
➤ In what way do you try and follow their example?

Buddhists show their respect for the Buddha in many different ways

A Buddhist shrine where Buddhists can meditate upon the life and teachings of the Buddha.

Long after the Buddha died, his teachings were written down. Many Buddhists read them today.

Mount Kailas, Western Tibet. A place where Buddhists like to make a special journey. It helps them feel closer to his life and teaching.

Monks in Ajanta caves in Maharashtra, India. After a long life of traveling and teaching, the Buddha died in the north of India. His body was cremated. His ashes were given to different rulers. Special monuments called stupas were built to mark where his remains were buried. Buddhists visit these places today to show him respect.

Buddhists in the 21st Century try to live as the Buddha taught

Buddhists showing their belief in peace.

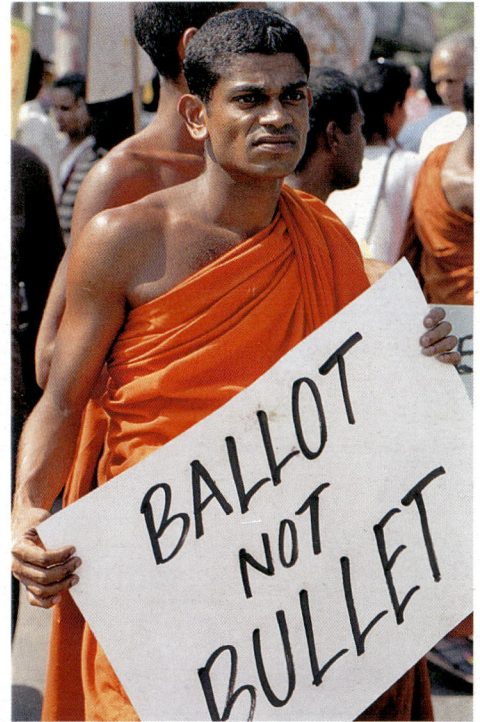

Buddhists are vegetarian. They do not believe in killing animals.

Buddhists showing kindness and helping people in prison.

STOP & Think ?

➤ What other special journeys do you know about where people go to show respect?

➤ Do you have a special symbol or object to remind you of someone important to you?

PAUSE & RECORD

• Look closely at the pictures on this page. Choose one and think of 5 questions you would like to ask about it.

55

What do you know?

❶ You have come across many new words in this unit. Copy the table into your books and fill in the blanks. The page numbers are there to help you.

Truth (page 51)	
Meditation (page 49)	
Dukkha (page 52)	
Enlightenment (page 50)	

❷ Look at the list below, which shows many of the important events that happened in the Buddha's life. Choose four of these and write them in your books in the order in which you think they happened.

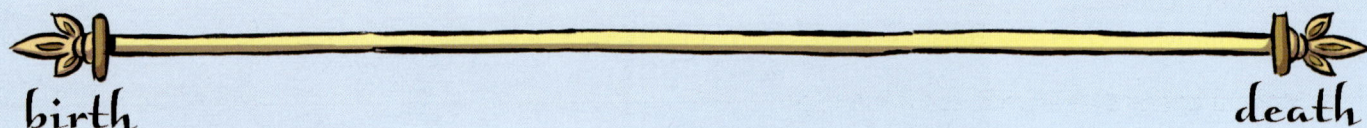

birth   death

becoming enlightened

leaving home and his family

seeing the four sights

being kept in the palace

seeking the truth

teaching about The Four Noble Truths

What do you think?

Look at the words listed in each of the lines A, B & C. One of the words in each line is out of place. Decide which ones they are. Draw a picture of a bin in your book and write the words which are out of place, inside it. Compare your bin with your partner and discuss any differences.

A	Role Model	The Buddha	Respect	God
B	Right Understanding	Right Action	Going to War	Right Speech
C	Illness	Someone young	Death	Old Age

action INTO

Choose from the following activities:

❶ Draw two eight-spoke wheels. In the first wheel, describe something in each spoke that changed in the life of the Buddha. In the second wheel, describe eight things that have changed in your life.

❷ Make a collage from pictures in newspapers and magazines. In one half use examples of greed, hate and envy. In the other half use images of peace and contentment. (You could include drawings and photos of your own if you wish.)

❸ Using the information in this unit and the website www.buddhanet.net/ devise a tourist poster encouraging people to visit **'Important places in the Life of the Buddha'**. By each place you will need to explain why it is important for Buddhists today.

Final thoughts

This unit has asked the question: Who was Gotama Buddha? You have learned that he discovered some important truths about life which he passed on to others. His discovery of these things is known as **The Enlightenment**. Write this word down the side of your page and see if you can find an important word in this unit which begins with each letter.

Samantha hatched beside millions of other salmon. She swam through the clear river. She was heading for the sea. She swam on past huge ships. She got to the sea. There were strange creatures everywhere.

Years passed. She felt like the river was calling her back. So she swam towards it. This was against the flow and so it was very hard. She wanted to get back to the river. Here she would make her own babies. She kept going. She was exhausted. Then... her way was blocked by a huge wall of concrete.

It was a dam. She tried to leap over it, but it was huge. She was too tired. She died, exhausted. The dam workers just got on with their work.

Dam!

Every time a dam is built there are winners and losers:

- Work for local people
- Electricity is made. This makes life easier
- Beautiful land might be destroyed
- People and animals might lose their homes

STOP & Think

➤ **Which two of these are good things and which two are bad things?**

The Big Issues

What might the problems be?

Climate Change

Every day, some of the sun's warmth is 'trapped' in the sky. This is called the **Greenhouse Effect**. If too much warmth is trapped, this could cause:

- more strange weather
- rises in sea-level
- changes in farming habits.

These could all harm life on earth. Climate change might be caused by:

Burning coal & oil (**fossil fuels**)

Using chemicals like **CFC's**.

Methane gas caused by cows passing gas.

These can all make '**greenhouse gases**'. These gases trap sunlight. This makes the earth warmer.

Resource Depletion

There are only so many natural resources. If we use them up, they'll run out.

- **Energy** comes from things like oil and gas. There's only so much in the earth.
- Other materials, like metal ores, will eventually run out.
- Things like wood need time to re-grow. These are called **renewables**.
- Some living things are **endangered**. This means they are close to being lost forever. This means there's less **biodiversity** (variety).

We need to learn to use things in a **sustainable** way so that we still have things in the future.

Pollution

Every time you go to the toilet you cause pollution! Some pollution has to happen, some doesn't. People who worry about the environment are called **environmentalists**. They think we should not cause pollution when we don't have to.

Ralph Archibald is a garden gnome. He is made out of plaster. This came from deep inside the earth. It was carried by dirty lorries to factories. Strange chemicals were added. He was baked in an oven using a **HUGE** amount of electricity. More chemicals were added. Then more lorries to the garden centre (cough cough). Sadly, one day he got broken. Never mind, he can be replaced.

Your Choice

Every time we buy something (and not something else instead) we make a choice. When something's good for the environment we call it 'environmentally friendly'. How often do you buy environmentally friendly things? Why should you?

Here are three sponges. Which one would you buy?

This is man-made using chemicals.

This is natural but cleaned up using chemicals

This is completely natural

STOP & Think

➤ **Which sponge is the most environmentally friendly? (See next page for hint.)**

PETROL CRISIS?

Britain 2000. Truck drivers weren't happy with the cost of petrol. They stopped tankers getting out of refineries. People were running out of petrol. This caused problems. So the government made petrol cheaper.

'We were right' If petrol's too dear people can't get to work. Buses are no good. You need a car.

'You were wrong'. People use too much petrol. This harms the environment.

Sponges: The completely natural one is probably best. The chemicals in the others probably harm the environment somehow. But, even the completely natural one is only good if it is taken from the sea very carefully. Not easy to choose is it?

action INTO

You are going to buy a fridge. Copy this list. Then cut each statement out. Put them in order. 1 = the thing which is most important to you when buying a fridge, 10 = the thing which is least important to you when buying a fridge. Discuss in groups.

a. The fridge looks nice.
b. It doesn't use much electricity.
c. It is very big.
d. It can make fancy ice shapes.
e. It uses environmentally friendly chemicals.
f. It is cheap.
g. It is trendy.
h. It is easy to keep clean.
i. It makes good ice-cream.
j. It is very quiet.

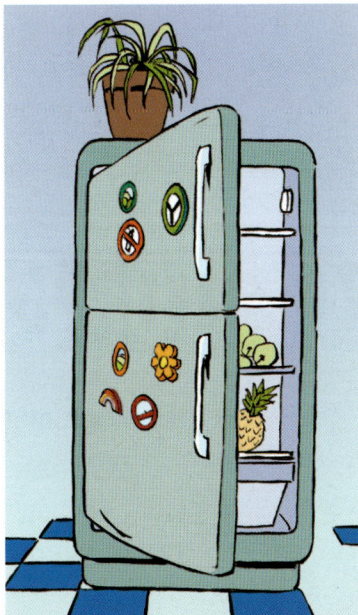

text message.........

Most bins are emptied every week. They usually have about 10kg of rubbish inside. Most of this is plastic. It is hard to get rid of and isn't very environmentally friendly. If it's burned or buried, the chemicals in it can get into the environment and cause harm. Silly, when we only use it to wrap things for a little while.

▮▮ PAUSE & RECORD ◉

• Find two newspaper stories about the environment. Stick them in your workbook.

61

Laurence is in prison. He's locked up all day. He'll never see his family again. His cage is his world. What has he done? Nothing! He's a lion and lives in a zoo.

Sally's got a cold. She won't get better. She'll be killed. So will her friends and neighbours. She'll be burned in a pile of bodies. She is a sheep and has foot and mouth disease – maybe.

Oliver has stood for 300 years. He's happy. He is a home for many creatures. He is nice to look at. He keeps the air fresh. Oliver is an oak tree. People love him. But he's going to be chopped down. He's in the way of a new motorway.

Human Responsibility

Humans sometimes behave towards nature in a strange way. There's 'Dolphin friendly tuna'. Who cares about the tuna?

We do things to other creatures that we don't do to people:

- we don't eat people
- we don't do scientific tests on people without asking
- we don't kill people because they're in our way
- we don't let some people live and others die for no reason.

But we do all of these things to other living things. Why?

STOP &Think

➤ Does the environment have rights? What rights?

➤ What would you say to Laurence, Sally or Oliver if they could understand you?

Why care for the environment?

Humans can think about the future. We can make plans. Humans are very powerful.

So... maybe it's our job to look after the environment. If we look after it, it might last longer. It might be in better shape. We'd have to treat everything fairly. This would mean using our power wisely. This is called **stewardship**.

Why should we care for nature?

- Nature has rights too. Other creatures have the right to live just like we do.

- If we harm nature, it might harm us back! Do something here, something happens there. All life on earth depends on each other. This is called **interdependence**.

Why do humans think that people come first?

CASE STUDY: THE CAR

Is the car the biggest pest on earth?

I hate cars. A quarter of a million people are killed by cars every year. There are 680 million cars. They cause lots of pollution. They use loads of energy. Wide areas of land are destroyed to build roads. For the environment, cars are just a pest!

I love cars. They give me freedom to go where I want, when I want. Cars don't kill people, bad drivers do. And buses and trains cause pollution too. Even if everybody used a bicycle there would be pollution. And accidents!

Don't ban cars. Just make them better for the environment.

action INTO

"All cars should be banned!"
Do you agree? Give two reasons for your answer.

5

WHAT ARE WE DOING TO THE ENVIRONMENT?

What would religious believers want to do about the environment?

Religious teachings about the environment

Many religions teach that everything on earth was made. God made it. We should look after the earth because it is God's. Some religions have stories about the creation. Some believers think these stories really happened. Others don't. They're just stories to help us understand.

Some religions do not think the universe was created. They think it has always existed. It had no beginning.

Islam – Judging everyone

Allah made a paradise called earth. He put a beautiful garden in it. He made Adam and Eve to live in it. They were supposed to look after it. Allah said, 'just stay away from that tree'. They didn't. They were punished. Allah sent messengers to try to make things up with people. He kept trying.

Allah made everything for a reason. Everything deserves a chance. If people don't give things a chance, Allah will judge them badly.

We can choose what to do, but we should be sensible.

Christianity – People are special

God made everything. The heavens and the earth. Plants and animals. He was very pleased with what he'd made. Then he made a man and a woman. He made them a bit like himself. He put them in charge of the earth. But the man and the woman didn't do what God told them. God was angry. He made their easy life hard. It wouldn't get easy again until man, woman and God made friends again.

Judaism – Everything comes from G-d

The Torah tells us that G-d created everything. He made the sun and moon. He filled the earth with life. G-d took dust and made a man. He gave him life with a single breath. G-d did this in six days and had a rest on the seventh. Adam and his wife, Eve were supposed to run the world for G-d. But they wanted to be in charge themselves. They blamed a snake, but G-d punished them anyway.

Hinduism – Round and round

Brahma makes the universe. Vishnu keeps it going. Shiva destroys it. All work together. The universe dies and is re-born, dies and is re-born. So does everything that lives in it. One story says that the universe is part of Brahma's body.

When did it all begin? When will it end? No one knows. All life is part of Brahma. One day it'll all be gone. Then it'll start again. Round and round in circles. Forever.

Sikhism – God is everything. Everything is God

God existed before anything else. He couldn't make another God. So he made the universe. Sikhs call God: ik ong kar. One meaning of this is: God, who created everything with great power. God made it all. Everything is filled with his spirit. So everything is special.

Buddhism – Always changing

Some people on a journey had a rest under a tree. Then they cut it down. The Buddha gave them a row. 'That tree helped you by keeping you cool, and you cut it down!'

Buddha didn't want to answer questions about how the world began. He wanted to make the world better now. Nothing you see lasts forever – even the universe. Everything's changing all the time. All living things try to stop being reborn. They're all struggling with life. You should help them, not get in their way.

❙❙ PAUSE & RECORD 💿

Copy the following statements. After each one write which of these six religions might make the statement. There can be more than one religion for each statement.

- God made Adam & Eve.
- God made all life on earth.
- God punished Adam and Eve.
- We should look after earth because it belongs to God.
- All life comes from Brahma's body.
- All life goes round in circles.
- Nothing lasts forever.
- You should help things which are struggling with life.
- Everything is filled with God's spirit, so everything is special.

Most people don't harm the environment on purpose. Sometimes they just don't think. Sometimes they make the wrong choices. Sometimes this is because they have different opinions to other people. Even religious people disagree!

Christians

1. God put me in charge of earth. I'm a steward. We shouldn't just think about ourselves. We should think about other living things too.

2. Yes God put me in charge. That means putting people first. Before we worry about the environment we should make up with God. Then everything will be all right.

Muslims

3. Allah will judge us. If we harm the environment he'll be angry. Everything is here for a reason. We should live in peace with all things.

4. But watch out! You might end up worshipping nature, not Allah. Only Allah can sort out environmental problems. Humans are too weak.

Jews

5. G-d made us like him. It's our job to care for the environment. If we spoil it, we've failed.

6. Yes, G-d has given us power over the environment. But we should use it to make human life better. How can you say that a fish is more important than a person?

Hindus

7. Everything comes from Brahma. Only Shiva should destroy it, not me. I'm part of nature too. If I harm it, I might pay for it!

8. Humans should just live good lives. They should try to look after each other. The environment should take care of itself. Nature is for us.

Sikhs

11. God is in everything. If I harm any living thing I harm God. We should treat the environment just like we treat each other. With kindness.

12. But if we care too much for the environment, maybe we'll forget about people. What if it's a choice between the environment and people? People should always come first. God would want that.

Buddhists

9. Every living thing is struggling through life. We're all trying not to be reborn. We should be kind to all life and help it – not get in its way.

10. But we should be careful. We can get too close to the environment. We shouldn't care too much or too little. If all we think about is the environment, then we ignore our faith.

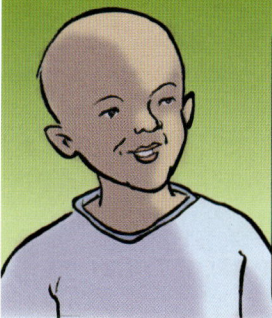

PAUSE & RECORD

1. Copy and complete:
   I **agree** most with viewpoint number ___.
   I think this because _____
   _____
   _____

2. Copy and complete:
   I **disagree** most with viewpoint number ___.
   I think this because
   _____
   _____.

What do you know?

❶ In your own words, explain why the story of Samantha the salmon is a sad story.

❷ From the following list, copy one thing which might *cause* climate change and one *effect* climate change might have.

- more strange weather
- burning coal and oil
- rises in sea-level
- cows passing gas.

❸ Here is a list of words/phrases and their meanings. copy them out and match them up.

Words/phrases

1. environmentally friendly
2. greenhouse gases
3. endangered
4. renewable energy
5. recycling
6. fact
7. opinion
8. stewardship
9. interdependence
10. dominion
11. creation

Meanings

a. gases which might warm up the earth
b. things which can regrow or replace themselves
c. the word religious people use for human power over earth
d. the word religious people use for humans looking after earth
e. a statement which you can easily prove
f. re-using things
g. a point of view
h. when things depend on each other
i. when something's close to being lost forever
j. the word used about how maybe God made the earth
k. when something's good for the environment

❹ Go back to page 64. Find the box about Christianity. Put the following events into the right order.

- God made the man and woman's life hard
- God put the man and woman in charge of the earth
- God made plants and animals
- God made a man and a woman
- God made the heavens and the earth.

❺ Draw a picture to go with each statement.

What do you think?

❶ Working in groups, produce a short information leaflet. This should be about an environmental problem. It should show what each of the religions on pages 64–65 would think.

❷ Make a classroom display of cuttings from newspapers about the environment. One side should show things we do to help the environment. The other side should show problems we cause.

❸ Imagine you are a follower of one of the religions on pages 64 and 65. You have been asked to join Greenpeace. Copy & complete the following:

I am a follower of [write religion here]. I will/will not join Greenpeace because [write your reasons here]

———————————————
———————————————
———————————————
———————————————

Final Thoughts

This unit has asked:

- What are we doing to the environment?
- Why should we care about it?
- What might happen if we don't care about it?

Answer the following:

In this unit:

❶ What have you enjoyed best?

❷ What did you not enjoy?

❸ How good was your work?

❹ What would you like to do better?

Now think of three questions about the environment that you still have.

action INTO

❶ **Interdependence** means that we depend on other things. The following list of people show the **connections** there are in getting a loaf of bread to your table. Choose two of the people and say who else in the list they need and why they need them. You'll need to think hard!

- farmer
- baker
- petrol producer
- shopper
- supermarket owner
- lorry driver
- electricity producer
- supermarket shelf-stacker
- bank manager
- doctor

❷ Do you think religious people should be more concerned about the environment than anyone else? Give at least three reasons for your opinion.

Index